WHATEVER'S FORBIDDEN THE WISE

ANTHONY MADRID

CANARIUM BOOKS
MARFA, NEW YORK CITY, ROME

WHATEVER'S FORBIDDEN THE WISE

Canarium Books
Marfa, New York City, Rome
www.canarium.org

The editors gratefully acknowledge
Columbia University School of the Arts
for editorial assistance and generous support.

Front cover:
Isidore Pils, *Drapery Study for a Bishop*.
Collection of the Metropolitan Museum of Art, public domain.

Back cover by Mark Fletcher.

First Edition

Printed in the United States of America

ISBN 13: 978-1-7344816-4-8

FOREWORD

The first nine ghazals here were written in the years 2012, '13, and '14. The last nine were written during the pandemic. Ghazals are marked with "†" in the Table of Contents.

People have asked me about the upright bar ("|") that occurs from time to time in the ghazals. Such bars indicate caesuras in places I thought might be counterintuitive, given the syntax of the sentences in which they appear. The idea was to make it easy to sight-read the poems gracefully, but the fact that I have to explain this shows I probably should just get rid of them.

The *rubāʿiyat* section is the first installment of what I hope will one day be a hundred poems. My model is Hālī.

The birthday poem for Roma includes authentic maxims culled from *Ashanti Proverbs* (Oxford, 1916).

The ANNEX section at the end, called *The Getting Rid*, appeared as a chapbook, June 2016, right before we moved to Texas. This section should be thought-of as a satellite to a short book called *Whatever's Forbidden the Wise*. The two texts are separate.

TABLE OF CONTENTS

THE GETTING RID

WHAT ARE THE THORNS OF THE ROSE

What are the thorns of the rose to the exploring ladybug?
Look how, from the proper perspective, the whole rose is petal.

Therefore, the proper perspective can never be that of a god.
You are strangely safe so long as you pick on | someone your own size.

You let fly an arrow, you should be content to let it fly.
You don't have to run alongside it and tell it how well it's doing.

You needn't promise it any reward; for when it has stopped in my neck,
it will have the same pleasure as comes from cinching a leather cord.

The heart's symbol is symmetrical: You scissor a folded sheet.
But the thing itself is as lopsided as a dog biting its side.

The heart's American eagle has its fingers spread out for flight:
it's as if our emblem for the human hand had a thumb on either side.

Madrid stands with the asymmetrical. He identifies with the writhing
snake
being inseminated by a feathered dragon on a cactus on the Mexican flag.

❧

ONLY THE BIRD SEES THE ELASTIC FILAMENT

Only the bird sees the elastic filament that tethers her to her eggs.
And even she does not see it with her eye.

So, let no one listen to admonitions regarding the shortness of life
from anyone who is not within sight of the end.

You cut a bamboo, want to drag it. You have to catch hold by the
   eyebrows.
For whoever lays hold on a wounded foot can expect to be kicked by
   the other.

You push off from the side of the pool? I push off from the air behind me.
You plunge and invert on encountering a wall. I disintegrate, turn into
   protein.

The world is full of ancient things whose shapes and colors have changed.
The beard of a Sumerian judge comes back as the braided neck of a
   coat hanger.

From the street I look through a glass door and see an ascending stairway.
And on the floor: a forest litter | of discolored fliers and coupons . . .

MADRID finds the words and joins them; someone else will be called
   the poet.
For how can we call him a poet, who is only a vase of crumbling ashes?

❧

IT IS WITH WORDS AS IT IS WITH PEOPLE

It is with words as it is with people: Actual beauty is rare.
We call things beautiful, not as such, but because of what they mean.

Because we commonly attribute beauty to whatever does us a favor,
we are reduced to puzzled despair whenever Actual Beauty says no.

Indeed, our calling a thing beautiful *almost* means it is not.
For how can we know it is beautiful until it betrays us?

A German sage once said "The trouble with these famous philosophers
is their only way of doing honor to an idea | is to say that it is true."

It is the same with words as it is with people: Actual beauty is rare.
Humiliated, we are no longer willing to *call* the beautiful beautiful . . .

MADRID is reading his poetry to a roomful of unearthed cultural relics.
He compares the white hair on their heads | to the flag that signals
    surrender.

❧

FOR THE FIRST TWO YEARS A PERSON'S WHOLE BODY

For the first two years, a person's whole body is a right-handed person's
  left hand.
Between two and six, the "left-handedness" is funneled into what's in
  fact the left hand.

The left-handedness coalesces there. Expelled from Paradise, it pitches
  camp.
And there it forgets it was instituted of God in the time of man's
  innocency.

It was, after all, instituted of God, so why must the mistake-making
  faculty
be always so ashamed, so ready to be punished? Why must it play the
  wallflower?

I was like Margery Kempe: I lay on my side to pray. I answered my
  husband
I would much rather die than consent to any "fleshly communing."

I would rather his head be struck off, or even for the world to end.
And if that's a mistake, it is mine; I can't be rid of it by cutting off a part.

Si tu mano derecha te hace pecar, córtatela y arrójala. My manner of prayer
was to listen to God—listen, and answer in tears. He said:—

I am not three. I am not a family. I am not a beautiful human face.
When you gaze at your painted Jesus, you have your back to me.

I reply: "Poor fool and knave, there's one part in my heart that's sorry
   yet for thee,"—
the fool being my left hand, and the knave my right. The evil-doer and
   the bungler . . .

&

A CELTIC KNOT WITH ITS LACES CINCHED

I balanced a sword on my head, dropped to my knees and earnestly
    vowed
I would never again APOLOGIZE on command.

I am done with Apology Culture, done with tendering and accepting.
If I'm commanded, I refuse; forced to listen, I stop my ears.

That place on the plate for the cup? that crater-like shallow socket——?
Its grip on the cup is comparable to my grip on social reality.

And if it doesn't always work? well! and why should we be surprised?
If it worked every time, you could hardly call it magic.

If it works every time, it's PHYSICS and contractual obligation.
A Celtic knot with its laces cinched can never be an emblem for magic.

And check out that fancy little fucker steppin' ahead there——!
The bestselling poet in America, with the morals of a drug addict.

And putting thát struggling cat in the hall is like trying to shove a bunch
    of feathers
into the roaring face of an auditorium fan.

The cat DEMATERIALIZES and reappears behind you.
Ungatherable, a galaxy of swirling feline hydrogen.

——And what do you think, Subhuti? Is this the pollution of the ideal?
——Bhagavan, by no means is this the pollution of the ideal.

For every bragging wretch, the world will hunt up an adventurous girl. Oh, you self-appointed trickster god, you will never lack a girl.

You'll never lack a girl, and lightning never lacks a target. ANATHA-MADRID has sent you a text message. It says *Don't get on that plane.*

❧

WE WOULD RENOUNCE THE SELF COMPLETELY

We would renounce the self completely, if only we knew it would "take."
We are willing enough to be nothing. We don't want to be a *residue*.

We look back on the Middle Ages and say they could not read.
One day *we'll* be somebody's Middle Ages; they'll say we could not read.

To be famous, to be talked about—these are like a Classical education.
One of those things we have to achieve, the better to renounce them.

The same thing that counts as a job well done | throws somebody else
out of work.
And for every scientific advance we have to pay | to junk the old
equipment.

"Savor pleasure and shun pain"—there's the old mistake.
For, why must we always scorn the plentiful in favor of the rare?

You wanna win every argument? Have a look at an onion.
For, the bricklayer of that minaret knew how to stack in perfect circles.

Show me no more equations, for I shall no longer discuss mathematics
with persons for whom solutions are found by recourse to numbers;—

Oh, when shall I ever be better understood than I am, right this moment?
RAFFI, try never! For only in the present moment have I found my reader.

❧

EVERY NUMBER'S A LIAR

If you had a million quarters, you'd have a quarter of a million dollars.
But a roll of quarters is just twenty bucks, and an empty hand is a debt.

We all love that classic story—not that we care about Christmas.
We like the idea that a man is his watch, and that a woman (his wife) is
    her hair.

If you are twenty-one today, kid, this is not your twenty-first year.
And this is your third, not your second decade. Get it? Every number's
    a liar.

You ask me if it rings a bell? It does. It does, but just barely.
It rings a bell the size of a Christmas light, on the other side of the
    parking garage.

I remember making a delivery, coming up a hill, and hearing sirens.
The other side of the road was a perfect rush-hour log jam;—

Suddenly, two ambulances blow by me, going the wrong way, on my side
    of the road.
Shot by me, to my right and left: they were driving on the wrong side
    of the road!

If I had been in either of their lanes, when those two ambulances crested
    that hill,
I would be molecules now. I'd be particles. And you, RAFFI, would be me.

❧

LIKE A CLOUD ABOVE A RAVINE

Like a cloud above a ravine is the hell you already know:
that sublime work of the imagination by Dante Alighieri.

But the rain that falls from that cloud is not made up of human souls.
It rains, and the rain funnels down into the something-other-than-human
sewer.

Look how a Chinese writing brush ends in a cone of rigid horsehair.
Loaded with ink, the cone will flex, will leave a wet trench in the rice
paper.

It will leave an attractive trench, and the daylight sucked into the ink
will give it a reflective "shine dot"—like looking into an animal's eye.

Which of you has looked into the looking-up eyes of a hair-trigger fox?
A backyard fox or a campsite coyote: Daoist, unintelligible, brave . . .

Which of you knows how *not* to part the pebble on the beach from its
colors?
The songbird from its social network? the fruit from its multifaceted
peel?

Oh, that sugary piece of phosphorus in its form-fitted velvet casing!
That ancient Egyptian sarcophagus meant | to be opened from the inside.

And each seed-bearing fruit has an atmosphere. Each has its several moons,
has tides (subject to gravity), changing weather, lunar eclipses . . .

But should an arrow suddenly snatch the waiting pomegranate out of
    your hand,
if it snatches the cap off your head, recall: its circuit has only begun . . .

For the arrow of the luckless archer returns to the middle of his or her
    back.
There, between athletic shoulder blades, is a diploma tube full of arrows.

Is a diploma tube full of arrows, and so | it is time for graduation.
The genie's gone back to his bottle; the devils to their fallow hells.

And the Chinese writing brush, and the cloud above the ravine (wherein
the charged particles have sorted themselves along their up-and-down
    axis),

and the looking-up eyes of the fox, and the sarcophagus, and the campsite
are irreducible to a system, are each of them floating over a void.

Truly: "All hells and hierarchies are works of the imagination." And
    equally:
"It is not the part of the Daoist sage to conjure meaningless hells."

ᚗ

DROP-MENU SCHEDULING CALENDAR WITH
ONLY ONE BLACK-OUT DATE

When he took me out with his people, you could see he was ashamed
   of me.
The next youngest guy there was twenty years older than I.

Observe the parent bird strangely urging | her babies from the nest.
The poet's eye is a mother bird, and the tears are jumping off his cheeks!

Come, Corydon, forget your Alexis. Forget Amaryllis's moods.
For this emphasis on sensual pleasure betrays your will to revenge.

The pursuit of knowledge is always a screen. Likewise, the asking advice.
People are poets. They just like to see certain themes being handled.

But if the artifact does not mean a thing until the maker is safely dead,
what are the audiences experiencing as I stand here and recite?

I have sixteen personalities, if each of my moods counts. And I
have no personality at all, if you're expecting consistency.

The serpent moves quickly, Palæmon. Its head is a den of thieves.
Look how the sentinels inside are slightly | parting the metallic curtains!

How appalling it is, in childhood, seeing that beautiful male brutes
quite frequently, without any study, are masters of magical speech.

How appalling it is, in childhood, to be so often made to admit
that the lethal force of language is in the keeping of the oversexed.

I have no last words nor any last wish. *Vive la différence!*
Oh, but Tityrus, before I go, let us share a bowl of wine.

Let us share a bowl, Tityrus. Your Melibœus must be on his way.
I'm off to the wrong airport: 4th of July, 2048.

᪷

NINETEEN GNOMIC STANZAS

The horse is suddenly vertical.
He almost stepped on a snake.
You are turning fourteen today;
it's Winter Break.

Whippoorwill or weeping willow:
one is a bird, the other a tree.
Archaeopteryx a-nesting
amid the debris.

Gray fox is the size of a cat.
His movements nobody knows.
Huangbo's first words to Linji were
"I forgive you thirty blows."

Three kittens live under that crepe myrtle.
A spider lives in the fronds.
Teacher loves asking questions
that don't have any response.

The snake's skin is made out of paper.
Its facets will sparkle and scintillate.
An alliance, the moment it's formed,
begins to disintegrate.

That tree has a jigsaw barkpattern.
Its fruit is a fluffy ball.
Rooster is big in his own place;
elsewhere, he stays small.

Elephant is her own shower head.
She has a career to pursue.
The stranger, at least, is impartial,
brings something new.

A bison will savor a dust wallow.
His motto is "Anything goes."
Have a look at the ants in the closet
eating your clothes.

The sea turtle scrambling seaward
has no time to figure his odds.
The vast majority of human beings
would never have invented gods.

The night sky is full of glitterers.
A centaur fleeing a scorpion.
Samuel Taylor Coleridge knocking
his fellow eater of opium.

Stately is the yellow-headed blackbird.
He stands on a stalk in the sun.
The taller the stack of incentives,
the less gets done.

Each oily black bug on its back
is a baby waiting to be changed.
You and the love of your life
are often estranged.

The Japanese yew is a spiky one.
She's impatient of any delay.
Six sunshines into July now:
It's a good day.

Buggy is the Texas night air.
I run out to cut me a switch.
When a devil goes to a funeral,
he lodges with a witch.

Here's a wintergreen field of sagebrush.
The roots are colorful corals.
Unwillingly we perceive nobody
has any morals.

Owl is a sullen contemplative.
He goes on a four-mile walk.
Three kittens live under that crepe myrtle:
Targets to eagle and hawk.

The iguana is a rocky planet.
He gets his heat from the sun.
The direction of consolation
is how you know who won.

The bull is an able attorney.
He can settle your case for a fee.
Archaeopteryx itself
a piece of debris.

Think they'll ever get it?
Time's up, and here are your scores.
Carpet-combing human being:
naturally on all fours.

❧

BIRTHDAY POEM FOR ROMA CADY MACPHERSON-WILSON, 2 JANUARY 2019, ÆTATIS SUÆ XV

On beauty we must pay a tax,
no matter how much we're earning.
If God gave the swallow nothing else,
he gave it swiftness in turning.

A boyfriend is a solemn thing.
His shirt and his shoes are mismatched.
In Ghana, Death is a skeleton, too,
but the ears are still attached.

Its ears are still attached, but that
does not mean *you* will hear it.
If you are an eat-by-myself type of girl,
you will not see a spirit.

Prizes are for the defeated.
Punishments go to the winners.
Leopard skins are rare, and so
are seldom worked by beginners.

The plumber has come with equipment
to undo the emotional clog.
The lizard does not eat pepper
and sweat break out on the frog.

If a rat gets a hold of a *fufu*,
he will eat it; he does not steal the pestle.
The souls of all tormentors are soft
like the lead of an artist's pencil.

A guitar is a hollow fruit.
Shake it and savor the sound.
Trees are a net: they stop bird bones
from ever reaching the ground.

Who stands wide awake in a darkened room
is apt to give people the shivers.
When a bird has a long enough bill, it has
no need of crossing rivers.

A boyfriend yields a lesson like
"The Death of Ivan Ilych."
A snake is like a rope, and yet
you don't use it to tie up a package.

You don't sit there making rope in front
of the animal you're trying to catch.
And no one teaches an Egyptian cat
to look in a calabash.

The Tathāgata never reflects.
The Tathāgata never thirsts.
By the time the fool has learned the game,
the players have dispersed.

❧

BABY SNAKE SIGNS WITH A FLOURISH

Baby snake signs with a flourish.
Her checkbook is any flat stone.
How many will benefit from the Teaching
cannot be known.

A male bison is a torn-up carpet.
A male bison is Wallace Stevens.
Saying "My guru is exempt"
releases demons.

The pelican in flight is a trash bag.
The fish, in a flash, is his diet.
The learnèd will never learn and cannot
be quiet.

The pecan tree is out of work now.
Her tears hit the roof of the bus.
If Mind and Buddha are intrinsically one,
why the fuss?

Stately is the yellow-headed blackbird.
He can stand on a blade of grass.
Your lecture may not be enlightenment,
but it'll pass.

Deneb is the swan's ass flap, yes,
and Rigel is Orion's foot.
"You should have nothing to do with ideas"
is nicely put.

The owl is an orchestral kettledrum.
Is a French horn with a button-down beak.
Of Patriarchs, Samadhi, Transmission
we ought not speak.

Underrated and under-serrated,
this lizard has a hazardous lip.
Who grabs the dharma with hot little hand
lets it slip.

Here's a wintergreen field of sagebrush,
twisted up at the foot of a fawn.
At the moment of Perfect Enlightenment,
Buddha's gone.

➷

BROWN BEAR IS A CONFIDING SCHOOLGIRL

Brown bear is a confiding schoolgirl.
She plays patty cake with a trout.
Beginners are always misled into
battling doubt.

The snows of Kilimanjaro.
The forest floor's under the covers.
The fact we're already enlightened
we learn from others.

This tree has a jigsaw barkpattern.
Has fruit and flower and fur.
The Perfected Being has no idea
which to prefer.

Owl is a sullen contemplative.
Her composure is evilly wrecked.
Bodhisattva, by definition,
does not reflect.

Three kittens live under that crepe myrtle.
Their way is to loll and retire.
You may wonder and ponder forever;
you may not inquire.

Rabbit will get his nine innings.
These nine will be like the last nine.
Venerating stupas, the Master said,
is a pastime.

The stag is a dashing hood ornament.
Is commonly thought an alarmist.
Tathāgata doesn't know squat
aside from the dharmas.

Kangaroo is an insulting marsupial.
She leaves her coat in the hallway.
Is enlightenment ever gradual?
Is it always?

Skunk family will amble in a herd.
They go slow, without any arguments.
Just like the scholar Fu Sheng
transmitting the *Book of Documents*.

৵

TUNGSTEN BUCKING BAR

Tungsten bucking bar. Riveting tale.
Swiss Army Knife glyph in a billy goat's eye.
The list of whatever's forbidden the wise
is, to my people, a menu.

Tungsten bucking bar. Change of venue.
Chamber enough for a swallow's nest.
They resected three inches of bone from my wrist:
like kicking away a kickstand.

Tungsten bucking bar. Drop it in quicksand.
Clock for the wind up, and caulk for the pitch.
Third time this week I have written a witch.
Kid, it must be Witch Week.

Tungsten bucking bar. Battle Creek, Michigan.
Candles in Lubbock, and cake in Des Moines.
I win the award and I helplessly join
the ranks of the overrated.

Tungsten bucking bar. Totally naked.
"The human race is a pile of sludge."—
Tallies well enough, undergraduate judge;
take care not to all-or-nothing it.

Tungsten bucking bar. Vitamin supplement.
Improved to within an inch of my life.
The bumblebee knows how to lick the knife;
The rose, how to wreck the bed.

Tungsten bucking bar. I looked overhead.
The sun was so bright I could see through the geese.
Molybdenum, nickel, and manganese
reversing repugnant and predicate.

Tungsten bucking bar. Corporal punishment.
Carpal weevils at work in their tunnels.
The hardhats are all coming back with their bundles
of fibers pulled off an orange.

Tungsten bucking bar. Don't be discouraged.
Just Corinth and Thebes and reasons for moving.
We have to stop telling ourselves we're im-
proving the people we punish.

❧

BAG OF BLACK BEANS

Bag of black beans. So try something new.
Set sail in a shoe, make a hole in the waves.
If I ever contribute to the world being saved,
it won't be for love of the people.

Bag of black beans. So run it by Legal.
Sealing a hole in the wall with a cork.
An artist's love is love for the work
as it *will* be when it's finished.

Bag of black beans. Norwegian and Finnish.
Adventurous curls and pitiful noise.
My *ahimsā* is the same as Tolstoy's,   अहिंसा
except he did it for God.

Bag of black beans. Aluminum rod.
Uruguayan sun with squiggling rays.
My *ahimsā*'s like MLK's,
except he did it for God.

Bag of black beans. Malfeasance and fraud.
I'm not into anger, I've taken a vow.
I get very angry, I'm angry right now,
but that's different from being *into* it.

Bracken and beans. Danish and Inuit.
The people in charge are following orders.
I mostly fail to give their supporters
the benefit of the doubt.

Bag of black beans. Porter and stout.
Le moyen age—*enfin* Malherbe.
I'm pledging myself to sharing the world
with people I cannot love.

Bag of black beans. White-wing dove.
When push comes to shove, when shove comes to *shove it*,
I'll tell you right now, you're not gonna love it.
You're still gonna have to share!

Bag of black beans. Like water, like air.
Filigree mesh of the trash receptacle.
Woe to the wonderful, curdling spectacle
of telling people off.

Bag of black beans. Gonna need you to cough.
The drooping vines will stand at attention.
Recrimination, recondescension,
this century's *soup du jour*.

Bag of black beans. We'll know for sure.
'Cuz each bean comes with a tiny white dot.
And as for the pricks, I'm done with that lot:
I've kicked all my toenails black.

❧

TEN RUBA'IYAT

Ruba'i

All lie awake, sweating and ashamed—
yet look at what they're ashamed of.
They're ashamed they didn't get their way, only that.
They're *the kind of person who doesn't get their way*.

❧

Ruba'i

Most people with their morals?
They're like the Martian who takes the lawnmower out of the box,
lays it on its side in the driveway, and stands back,
waiting for the grass to get shorter.

❧

Ruba'i

There's that blanket of iridium, sixty-six million years down.
Above that stripe: no dinosaurs.
"The enemy is not worth saving" is that iridium,
and I am one of the dinosaurs, dying off.

❧

Ruba'i

The camera is only interested in the beautiful;
the novel, in the young.
I want a new novel, a new camera:
the trans-tabletop demotion of sex.

❧

Ruba'i

People understand sensual pleasures.
About those, even children speak well.
But as to all other forms of human satisfaction,
people, to listen to them talk, have no experience.

❧

Ruba'i

If you bend a wire, but not too much,
something in the wire stays straight.

Wire knows what it was, remembers.
So it can go back.

❧

Ruba'i

Whoever has committed a crime
has "gone" when it wasn't their turn.
Now it's our turn.

Cruel, evil, it wasn't their turn...
When it's your *turn*, you can be cruel as you like.

৵

Ruba'i

I love Alexis de Tocqueville,
for he wanted a world in which a person like him,
for all his virtues,
would have no part.

৵

Ruba'i

One is trying to get something out of a coat pocket
without first removing one's glove.
Soon enough, one gives up, strips the hand:
to liberate its precision.

So, too, at death: one "strips the hand"—only,
it is the hand itself that comes off.

৵

Ruba'i

You are sitting on the corner of a pillow.
The pillow corner is under your thigh.
Almost unconsciously, you take away the pillow:
the relief is strange. It was worse than you knew.

So, too, at death,
we "remove the discomfiting pillow."
The thigh itself.

&

TWO BIRTHDAY POEMS FOR NADYA IN THE STYLE OF THE SHIJING, 5 NOVEMBER 2020

1

Gray fox bouncing at bugs
has small love of company.
My love, as no one will see her,
has ceased to dye her hair.

Gray fox crossing the sidewalk
has no time for gossip.
My love, as no one will find her,
must labor to find herself.

Gray fox ducks into the bramble,
is much loved, though never approached.
My love, seeking satisfaction,
endeavors to purchase a house.

੩੬

2

On the four-mile walk is a scorpion—
the size of eyebrow tweezers.
His whole life, he goes around half-cocked
and playing the world like a piano.
Not that he can play the piano,
but his scampering is like that.

On the four-mile walk is a deer herd—
sometimes surprisingly casual.
Their whole lives, they go around hair-triggered,
yet calmly look for their contacts.
Not that they look for their contacts,
but their eating is like that.

On the four-mile walk is the baby possum—
perhaps abandoned by Mama.
He has the littlest gleamers,
and less than a half hour to live.
Not that we know what will happen,
but the owls around here are like that.

On the four-mile walk is a girlfriend.
She brings with her her helpful friend.
They have many worries, must plan their classes,
yet feed each other fresh-baked bread.
Not that they feed each other bread,
but their comforting each other is like that.

❧

THE CHICKEN SITS DOWN, THE CHICKEN

A poem for little kids

The chicken sits down, the chicken.
And when she gets up, there's an egg.
Whoever gets under a table
is sure to encounter a leg.

The pony trots up, the pony.
She stops at the barnyard fence.
Whoever ascends a dining-room chair
can see all the way to Koblenz.

The kitten is needy, the kitten.
She's lapping up milk by the quart.
The couch's cushions are missing,
'cuz someone is building a fort.

The piglet is pleasant, the piglet.
He follows his friend down the path.
Who sits in a tub with her clothes on
isn't planning on running a bath.

The cows in the pasture, the cows.
Their equity lies in their udders.
The person of many collections
becultivates multiple clutters.

The turkey, indignant, the turkey.
He's stalking about in the yard.
Whoever insists on the easier task
must sometimes encounter the hard.

The snake in her jacket, the snake.
She does rather well with her hands tied!
A mountain of markers and pencils
must eventually end in a landslide.

The snake in her sweater, the snake.
She's hardly in need of a mitten.
Who trifles with neighborhood dogs
will enter the ranks of the bitten.

The mouse in the kitchen, the mouse.
The nibblers are nibbling the spinach.
The person who's learning to skateboard
will soon be in need of a bandage.

The swallow a-nesting, the swallow.
Her home is a sculpture of mud.
Who peels away bandage and scabbage
will go toe-to-toe with the blood.

The rat on the rafter, the rat.
He travels with horrible accuracy.
And the children in line for their haircuts
are helping along the democracy.

❧

INDIFFERENT TO THE PART OF THE DAY OF WHICH
SHE OUGHT TO BE SYMBOLIC

INDIFFERENT to the part of the day of which
she ought to be symbolic,
Vulture works mornings, never graveyard,
brains cool as an astronaut's...

Meaning night is better than day.

WITH regard to skunks, whenever I perceive
the smoky odor of spray,
I affect indignation, clucking concern,
and say: *Who's been annoying my friends?*

Meaning loyalty entails pretending.

EAST Texas tarantula, high-kicking chorus line,
strutting the afternoon asphalt,
would happily surround a cricket
and kick him into the fan blades.

Meaning the other end of a leg is a mouth.

LIVING lizard, wrong place and wrong time,
fated to be broomed out of sight,
so the sensitive can come up the sidewalk
without discouragement...

Meaning whoever has nothing gives more.

SQUIRREL grips oak tree, upside down,
    tail lashing like the string of beads
that tethers a pen to a countertop. Squirrel's
upside down; his head isn't.

Meaning confession is incomplete.
Meaning something is held in reserve.

IN our headlights, down in the hollow,
    where all channels lead to the river:
a dog on its spine, flapping like a bag.
It rights itself—strikes battle stance.

Meaning good and bad meet in a hinge.

CALM cat in the road does downward dog.
    It looks a luxurious stretch.
But in Ghana they say if cats really liked it,
they'd stretch all the way to Europe.

Meaning pleasure requires a codebreaker.

NIGHT fence, street lights, sluggish possum.
    Tail, other side of the fence.
Four little hands, knuckles visible.
"Resting unimpressed face."

Meaning malice is bioluminescent.

M AMA muskrat, leading two little footballs,
     making paths through long grass, down
to their drainage-canal, intrauterine, hide-
away home-under-a-highway.

Meaning pockets are nature's pottery wheel.

W HAT happens to a deer's whitetail legs
     when it lies down in the whitetail grass?
A deer is a metal folding-chair:
parts collapse out of existence.

Meaning license revoked, things vanish.
Meaning you have to have a *license* to exist.

K ILLDEER are known here as "ninny birds,"
     for the offensive and chickenistic way
they passive-aggressively scold and sass back,
scattering in retreat.

Meaning wise words come out of cowardice.

ৎ➤

LIKE THE ROOTS OF A TULIP POPLAR

Collaboration ghazal, written with Ana Sweeney

A dream is like the roots of a tree: like the roots of a tulip poplar,
whose searching filaments cannot but take hold of whatever they
    encounter.

The piccolo is a mighty instrument, mightily misunderstood.
For a high note is a well-aimed arrow, and a trill is a circular saw.

A dream and the roots of a tulip poplar are CELLS of the insurgency.
They work in darkness, in dark detritus, and issue their challenges
    upward.

Ad libitum is a lie. For, whoever looks away from the score
is merely following a music she does not understand.

Look, an upended poplar's roots! A dream, taken out of context.
But the piccolo, put back in its case, is *removed* from its natural setting.

Every day, my lungs fill with water, just as if my hollow body
were a conch shell or a ruined ship, returned to the boiling sea.

No dream is uninhibited, Ana. Yet, know the inhibitions issue
not from morals, but from the properties of the soil.

᠁

THE INFINITELY LONG NEED NOT BE WIDE

The infinitely long need not be wide, nor the infinitely harmonious audible.
Infinities, on the whole, have | a tendency to disappoint.

Sickness is a myth, pain is a hypothesis: such was my father's philosophy.
He was of the generation that ruined us. And I'm not grateful.

You are polite to my face; behind my back, it's something different.
Don't think you're freer back there, where you must coddle and deceive.

Adam and Eve and the crocodile were harmonious from the start. It's not
their differences that caused the disaster, but the ways they were the same.

So, envy me, you whose lovers are willing. For, suspended in a state of
   despair,
a HUSBAND finds (for himself and his bride) the bubbling Fountain of Youth.

The pulse in the diamond's lymph nodes cannot be perceived by sensualists.
But the pure of heart can hear the thoughts of the eels in the Gulf of
   Mexico.

My sovereign said I'd be paid in gold, for every verse I composed.
And then paid again in gold—and something more—for every verse I
   struck out.

Chop chop, MADRID. Which verses will you cut? And which can you
   not bear to?
What ransom, Malek osh-Shuʿarā, these inaudible harmonies?

࿎

THE ROOT NOT WHERE IT SHOULD BE

I am resisting the urge to curse you, my student.
But it's like holding a tarp over a struggling animal.

Minimal is my concern with stolen kisses.
Let the brokerage and the Board of Directors tabulate losses.

I hate all cops and bosses. Parents and teachers too.
Whoever has an advantage, whether they earned it or not.

As for our anxiety, we dare not strike at the root.
For, the root (not where it should be) is the head itself.

What's best? Not to make a list, but to feel like making a list.
Not to kiss and caress, but to feel like it.

Yet, I hate all honey badgers, trash-rooting rats and raccoons,
all human demi-beings with no sexual insecurities…

—"Go die, Madrid! since you don't know how to live."
—Madrid says: "Fine, I'll die."

And now I'm a ghost, the ghost of myself,
and permitted to speak from the Void.

8

IS IT SAFE TO WALK ON A ROOF'S EDGE

What is your goal, young person? A world wherein the Evil
are shackled to the wall, humiliated, left to writhe——?

But then they simply lie in wait, watching their opportunity to strike.
And it's not like they'll never get that opportunity…

Is it safe to walk on a roof's edge? If you are a cat, yes.
Is it safe to walk on the edge of a roof? If you are a drunk, no.

Go now, bird, where it's safe to walk, and ask no one's advice.
Take no heed of the starter bees' nest with only one bee on it.

Indeed, you are no goddess, for you are subject to rotten luck.
Nor are you quite the princess, though people dread your displeasure…

Can a stone be used as a sponge? Surprisingly, yes.
But it is like when lovelorn people come asking advice.

A perfume will evaporate right through the stopper, it's true.
But the water in the stone can never get through to its nucleus.

Fit a pencil in the gutter of a book, one end out the bottom.
Put your thumb on the end, and lever it up into your fingers,——

and add a note to the margin of these modular strophes, Alexis.
For whatever you write in this book is bound to improve it.

৺

ABOUT WHERE TO BUILD

There is good and bad, better and best, when it comes to where to build
 a nest.
About where to build, a swallow has many ideas…

Black tea is as good as it gets. Tea with a pour of goat's milk.
That milk will descend the atmosphere, billowing like a ghost.

Most poetry translations are hairless cats. Apparently nobody minds,
as long as the wadded blob of elbow skin says *meow*.

How say you, Fragment of Feeling? Do you recognize yourself
in the guise of a KOMMISSAR whom nobody dares reproach?

Texas Cockroach will come and take | the spoon right out of your hand,
will look you dead in the eye, and lick the spoon.

Last July, I skipped the fireworks. No, it's a lie! I saw 'em.
I saw 'em reflected on the houses across the street.

Wheat bread, cut for a sandwich. Onions, thick as your hand.
Rock-hard fungus at the foot of the steps. The "leaves" of painted wood…

And now my spirit is happy. *Ya no puede caminar.*
I bet I know whose birthday is tomorrow.

Thoughts black, hands apt, drugs fit, and time agreeing:
MADRID, attempting to turn himself | back into a human being.

❧

WHEN A FIBER GETS CAUGHT IN A NIB

When a fiber gets caught in a nib, you go from extra fine to double broad.
That is being in love: you get a hair caught in your nib.

As long as I live, I shall be the boy who bought a whip and cracked it.
There was a particular leaf on a bush: I saw it *vaporize*.

Sitting on the floor in a melting apartment, we waited for the poets to
    begin.
With a piece of ragged cardboard, I fanned | a stranger with her back
    to me,—

and she (we had exchanged no words) lifted her ponytail out of the way!
What could the poets add to this scene? Only the word *vaporize*.

But now, a cinnamon tree in the moon and the rabbit who hides there
are the confidantes of my heart, as I lie here, waiting.

I'm older now. One day I'll be so old that, on entering a conference
    room,
I'll have to turn and draw my beard in after me, before I close the door.

A lob in tennis is a southbound parabola. A set of sharp turns is a cube.
My body's career in the world of the senses is a pill, crushed in a mortar.

Swamp oak, back of the house! Wood louse under the floor! For what
am I searching this U of C reprint of *The Edicts of Aśoka*—?

Put a mark on the floor where MADRID is to stand, and give him the
   signal to begin.

Then, one by one, he will bend a set of horseshoes straight, with his
   mind.

&

PLAYS WITH FIRE SHOULD SAVOR SMOKE

You are not the source of your shadow—though I allow it matches your
    outline.
You are no SPOOL OF STRING, whose Shadow issues from Self.

A spool of cotton string, with its woven pattern—!
Those overlapping diamonds, losing layer after layer…

Betrayer of Self and Soviet, who taught *you* to shred a diamond?
Who taught you to treat the *passengers* as ballast?

Working fist and phallus: the Corrupter and his Pupil.
Plays with fire should savor smoke, Lucien Chardon.

'Cuz smoke is fire's shadow. This fountain pen, a jet.
This Texas snail, a glue gun | or a roll of masking tape.

But all those landfill ballpoints? They are compass needles, pointing
to the MAGNET that will melt them in our lifetimes.

To underline every line in the book, you have to *soak* it in ink.
The Dao knows all about that. It underscores; it also strikes out.

DICKINSON was braver; she told the gunman to blow her head off.
But if you pull the trigger on a Texas snail, all you get is bubbles…

As a poet, MADRID was the jazz they play through the phone when you're
    on hold.
The stuff one hums to oneself while folding laundry…

Anodyne toodle-oo jazz that can't hold a shape
any more than can a moon-negative of a tulip.

❧

I HELPED A BOY WITH HIS TEST

Live oak is not earth, is not displaced soil. Oak appears unprompted,
as do suns, and planets, and lovers—and hatred of the old for the
    young.

A nest of swallows appears unprompted in a downward-pointing vent.
The eggs, the mud, the excrement fit that vent like a key in a lock.

But whoever builds an enclosure pulls a string on a silver bell,
which summons those outside the enclosure to a sullen act of predation.

Here's a moth with a wintergreen parka. She leaves prints, walking up a
    pen.
Trapped under a funnel all night, she cries | correction fluid onto the
    table.

Many are the things that can be learned but not taught. Evil, that the
    teachers
of those things receive the same honors as everyone else.

I helped a boy with his test; he passed, and leapt into my arms!
Two-hundred-pound kid, all tungsten muscle, climbing me like a tree…

With *my* bad back, I was scared, but I found that a boy whose soul is light
weighs no more in your arms than his empty clothes would, if *they* were
    flung into your arms.

❧

YOU HAVE TO THROW SOME AWAY

To eat the fudgsicle without tasting the stick? You have to throw some
    away.
With regard to the belovèd's body, it's the same. If you have it all—you
    taste the stick.

To be menaced by a pool full of girls will prevent your passing that way
    ever again, boy.
Yet, look how you've tracked through the rings of Saturn, avoiding that
    one neighborhood pool.

From any point on a turning sphere, one should be able to see the whole
    room, and yet,—
there are stars we can never see in this hemisphere: the Earth, always
    in the way.

Tears, too, are only round in flight, and perhaps they too are spinning.
Each with its Magellan on a mission that can only end in a splash.

If CLEANSING is the natural purpose of tears, doesn't that clearly show
that the body believes being *upset* is a form of pollution?

What comes out of a tarantula is also silk, could be made into cloth,
    would be priceless.
A blouse of it would have something in common with minnows changing
    direction.

There *is* such a thing as very rough silk—they use it on the outside of
    boxes,
the inside of which is normal soft silk, full of waves, like a tub of
    mercury.

The male housefly strokes the female's head, prior to copulation.
How does he know to do it? and how does she understand?

All his life, MADRID has been stroked on the head, prior to copulation.
Yet, he is no female fly, for he—has never understood.

❧

THE GETTING RID

OFFLINE PIECES

2013–2015

HERE IS ARTY VERONICA

Here is arty Veronica
With her colicky rag of hair.
Electric guitar, harmonica
Are harbingers of despair.

The monkeypriest and the poopycup
Were stupid with admiration.
They stood too close and got fucked up
By the rep from Aryan Nation.

Monkey see, monkey write.
Colin Clout's come home again.
But blood is not ink despite
Your feeding it through a pen.

Daughter, where is your dog collar?
Where are your whips and plugs?
I don't know why I bother
Policing these little thugs.

The little door in my chest
Is opening and out comes a ladder.
And the monkeypriest and the poopycup
Are oozing out like batter.

I'm just mad about Saffron.
Saffron's mad about me.
Pseudoepinephrine in
A tiny white cotton T.

Listen as Teacher scolds me.
You'd think I hadn't a prayer.
But after school she told me
To come but I was already there.

Oh, bell without a clapper!
Oh, new sud in the rinse!
You can't expect these rappers
To come to their own defense.

Oh, Alpha Zulu Foxtrot!
And, thanks to the god of wealth,
I'm sick of all these doctors.
Physician, fuck thyself.

In the depths of the walk-in closet,
Women are young men too.
With the help of a safety deposit
We can all hopple on through.

I caught Veronica sexting.
She's carrying on like a stallion.
I trust the story is extant
And written in choice Italian.

Praise! It don't come cheap.
You're apt to lose your Zen.
But all the literati keep
Eleemosynary friends.

If you haven't seen the photo,
Better give Baby his bottle.
She is a shocking babe. Hakuna
Matata, Nezhukumatathil.

Poet, supplant the porn!
Conjure the gorgeous ass.
'Til teenage boys all scorn
These corny photographs.

Father, accuse not your son.
The son who loves you so.
The poopycups will come.
They have nowhere else to go.

The monkeypriests are approaching.
They bring their terrible sword.
You cannot resist the power of
The poopycups of the Lord.

And Veronica isn't human.
Whom she does not love she hates. I eat
The cunt of a brutal woman
And I don't care how long it takes.

I don't care how long it takes!
Let it go on 'til Hanukkah!
This is the United States.
And this is arty Veronica.

❧

LISTENING TO "VICIOUS"

Listening to "Vicious"
And trying to forget
The hole whence issues
Miles of curling shit,

I heard it crackle into existence:
Le grand peut-être.
And up ahead in the distance:
Shimmering Kamasutra.

The coming of the white man?
That was the first heave.
Relax, said the overnight man.
We are programmed to receive.

Rita's out feeding the meter.
I hope she took her card.
For consigned to the end of a needle
Is the holoblastic canard.

Holly's gone back to Miami.
Arrived there on a yacht.
Wasn't 'til later the Sugar Plum Fairy
Came and hit the slots.

KIT MARLOWE knows the tune!
And knows just how to pilot
A Montgolfier-style balloon
In the atmosphere of Titan.

But who can tell what Maisie
Said before she swooned?
These women all go crazy
'Bout a sharp-dressed wound.

But the candyass in a tux
Is starting to whine and pester:
"I don't want to be a *bitch*?
But she's gained a lot of weight this semester."

You did it, not me.
So who deserves the punch?
X.Y.Z.P.D.Q.E.D.,
As soon as I pop the clutch.

I have to squat to pray.
Oh, my offense is rank!
James Dean for a day,
But eventually Hillary Swank.

Way ahead of you, Marge.
No ideas but in things.
I just want to practice my art.
The tension in the strings,

The anxiety in the air,
And the six rows of teeth—
Did it all on a dare
And slid right into its sheath.

So much for making it with a sexy.
No more chin than a rat.
Placebo, *dilexi*,
But we don't talk about that.

And in the CAPTAIN's chambers
They gathered for their Faust.
Quiet! you'll wake the neighbors while we're
Burning down their house.

Hablaba como niño
In my mu gu gai pan. I had to
Watch those girls from the video
Stab it with Steely Dans.

But the Suicide Bomb Fairy
Ain't out to make it new.
Addicted to dairy
And to the cutting through.

And I reflected on my suction
In the snow-covered hills:
Exploded perfection
Through a rolled-up dollar bill.

And if the real thing don't do the trick?
Arrepientete, chica desnuda.
Give it a double click.
Ooo. Barracuda.

❧

ONCE UPON A TIME

Once upon a time,
There was a beautiful shark.
She combed her long, blonde hair,
And it made the halibut bark.

It made the chicken oink,
And the whale to run for Congress.
A man should never obstruct
The course of material progress.

Yet a lamb cannot but weep
When the kiddies come home from college.
For they have forgotten to keep
The agreement they made to acknowledge

The woodpecker's right to peck,
And the maple's to be pecked at.
Let's have a little respect
For Rubber Duck with a doctorate.

That provocative way of standing!
All elbows and bangles
And hips just like a coat hanger
And ankles at right angles! I like

The shape of the pouring soymilk,
The sound of the splitting log.
But Egret finds it regrettable that her
Sister is dating a dog.

Don't listen to 'em, kid!
And don't listen to their questions.
This corporation's been ruined by
Well-meaning false confessions.

And the world is fast a-melting,
Though I would have it slow.
And I don't think it's helping:
The way these animals go

Straight from hatchery to quackery,
And, if only to amuse,
I'll throw my hat in with Mike Thataway in
Black patent leather shoes.

Maybe I'm just like my mother.
She's never satisfied.
Maybe I'm just like my father:
Always a bridesmaid, never a bride.

Maybe I'm just like my cat:
Licking invisible balls.
Perhaps you'll reflect upon that,
Next time you're screening your calls.

And all the solvent and the solute,
They were walking hand in hand.
This, the Indian poets were
The first to understand.

The ancient Indian poets
Had their heads screwed on straight.
Fixed on the body's affluence
And the effluents that escape.

And the influence they enjoyed?
Close-focus hocus-pocus.
And every *gezunte moyd*
In a juvenile honey locust

Will prefer their Hindi distichs
To the Indiana Hoosiers.
We're gonna be there from Spit Christmas
All the way to Mucus New Year's.

But for now I draw the curtain
And settle into Lent.
Last person to go to Harvard
Without knowing what that meant.

ॐ

PRETTY LITTLE FAILBOAT

The poems in that book suck bug nuts.
I believe you know the drill.
I must find the woman Cabrera, sleeves
Cut at a chevron angle.

Today I am a ladybug.
I'm sitting on a policeman's shoulder.
I must find the woman Cabrera:
Thousand bucks says you miss.

At the *Cena Trimalchionis* I saw
Two poodles in a yard.
Why don't you run off to your little hidey-hole,
And think that one over.

Sucks to suck, my poo nugget.
I'll do whatever you say. Oh, *look*
Where attention-deficiently
The poor wretch comes reading!

To a perpetual state of hiphop
And an organ-grinder God,
SACHER-MASOCH hath no ear: to that
High requiem become a Sade.

Here is something new.
I can turn myself into a ladybug!
Can put on a bolero jacket
And take a vacation.

With pen uncapped, I'm turning the leaves
Of the entomological dictionary.
I hate every single poet who's
Not in my generation.

I ain't looking for an apology.
I'm runnin' up my phone bill,
Standing out here in snowshoes
In the nick of Nova Scotia.

Mister Button-on-a-Trumpet!
Miss Bellybutton with a gem!
I'd like to see something in writing. Guys
Love it when you boss 'em around.

Guys love it when you boss 'em!
So step up and voice your demands.
The Asian skunk cabbage blossom
Took part in the show of hands.

And Rachel Rip-Roarin' Masterson's
All over the room at once.
A NAVAL ORANGE who's out to encourage
The drill, the saw, and the punch.

The drill, the saw, and the punch!
I know, I know, I know. We gotta
Save her before she flunks,
The pretty little failboat.

Is a flowerpot a kind of flower?
Or only a kind of pot? I am
Fucked and getting fuckeder. I'll
Do whatever you say.

Here is something new.
I'm running lines in a corner. I must
Find the woman Cabrera, I must
Turn myself into a ladybug,—

I must defeat the disinclination
Of the two poodles in the yard:
Hunt up a tragic marker
When it's time to sign the card.

And if, fackity fack, she turns her back,
I know how to get 'er done.
Take a bicycle pump to a Moonbounce,
Sink a shovel in the sun.

A shovel in the sun! Oh,
I do whatever I'm told! Seventeen
Stanzas for the klepto, seven-
Teen-and-a-half years old.

❧

PEACH PEACH PEACH

Peach, peach, peach
And a pickle in the car
Nichaelmas, Michaelmas
Rah rah rah

Wichita, Wichita
Whudja wanna do
They try to find a reason while
They ride the kangaroo

With a teeny girl, teeny girl
Falling in between
And Heidegger and Husserl
'll hide the magazine

With a Chickasaw, Chickasaw
Chapanese sword
Ya got a chicken with a Choctaw
Writin' on the board

And a ballyhoo, ballyhoo
Babblin' away
Like an ocelot that talks a lot
To Mr Mallarmé

And a mop-along, pop-along
Howdja like me now
We're goin' to the gamelan
That mama don't allow

With a nicotine, nicotine
Nip it in the bud
Nanofirst and nanosecond
Nano-fuckin'-third

A-with a nanny goat and au pair
Never goin' home
We are hoggin' all the tapenade
And talkin' on the phone

Like a Lee, Lee, Lee
And a Deuteronomy
We are doing unto others
What they doing unto me

Like a Chicu-chicu cheek-cheek
Ready on the set
Relegate the television
To the bassinet

Marmoset and marmalade
Are martyrin' the dude · Oh!
How we gonna execute
Without exactitude · Oh!

Troubadour, troubadour
Truman on the air
With a Cuban toucan so that you can
Tell he doesn't care

Like a matriarch, matriarch
Making up the rules
We are messing with Vanessa in the
Fountains and the pools

Port 'n' starboard haven't harbored
Half as many men before
Didja make it to Jamaica
Ordja have to come ashore? Row, row, row,

Roman à clef, roman à clef
And Roma turnin' ten
Her mama singin' rondolet
We sing it once again

With a BIG peach, peach
And a pickle in the car
Nichaelmas! Michaelmas!
RAH RAH RAH

&

PANTS PANTS PANTS

Pants, pants, pants
And we're bouncin' off the walls
And Peter Rich'll teach ya which
Ya beach- and basketballs

Ya beach- and basketballs
Ya slam 'em in the net
HELL sinky! kinda kinky
Key to *Oubliette*

Umma-gumma yes, ma'am
Oh m'God, no
There's the siren, Keats and Byron
Tie! it's time to go

Guy, it's time to go!
'Cuz we're bouncin' off the walls
Like a rimshot Abbottabad
Ya beach- and basketballs

Ya kitchykitchy coo
Ya got a lot to do
And Bone-a-beck and Schoonebeek
Have found the fella who,

With a Walla Walla weedwhack
Whack-a-mole stick, said:
"You're a goner, Weimaraner."
Stop! I'm getting sick!

Ticklebug, Ticklebug
Quotin' up a storm
And Lollygag and Pantyhose
Are kinda getting warm

With a tabbernack, grabbernack
Tabulate the bill
They try to give Manhattan back
To Crackerjack and Jill

Boutonnière, boutonnière!
Buddha bourguignon
And the Taliban and Yes-We-Can
'll tell ya whatcha won

While the Wannabe and Wonton
Are walking on the bridge · They
Took a little jaunt on
The way to gettin' rich

Like an ixodid, ixodid,
Ixodid tick · Rocky
Mountain spotted fever with a
-pherson and a Mac-

On your mark get set you're dead
Arizona Schoonebeek
'Cuz the powderpuff has had enough
Of pounding on ya neck

And the Maki babe, khaki babe
'll pile 'em up and, oh!
The baby gotta incubate
Vagina dynamo

Aw c'mon, it's time to go!
With the chicken and the chicks
And the clock, clock, clock
And ya tockin' to the ticks

Like a pants, pants, pants
Let it echo down the halls
'Cuz we're getting in the barrel
Gonna reckon with the Falls

Gonna reckon with Niagara
Gonna kick it in the balls
Singing PANTS PANTS PANTS
While we're bouncing off the walls

❧

FOUR FOUR FOUR

Four, four, four
There's a dolphin on the floor
And a little jellybean
And a Delly-delly-phine

And a camisole Camille
When the camels start to squeal
When you're four, four, four
Who could ask for any more?

Quarter mile, quarter mile
Howdja like me now and how's ya
Bibbinism, Bibbinism
Miaow, miaow, miaow

This disturbin' university
And bourbon ingenue
With a Bibbinism, Bibbinism
You, you, you

But the Galahad, Galahad
He gotta get a job · I'm
Coming from la Mancha, cantcha
See the demagogue

Cantcha see the Commie Tommy gun
Is toppin' off ya tank
And the Wangbang and Nackanack
Have no one left to thank

And then they stack it up, back it up
And jackin' up the car · They are
Often soften-coughin'
All the way to Zanzibar

With a marzipan orangutan
A Mangapwani zoo
And the Sultanate insulting it
Interpret as you do

And the Kachyderm, Pachyderm
'll pat 'em on the back
'Cuz they runnin' up the credit card
A cricket on the track

And the Clabber Girl, Clabber Girl
'll clap 'em all in chains
Like a flak-jacket, try-to-crack-it
Buddha for your pains

Puppeteer, Puppeteer!
Pop him in the nut
'Cuz the Galahad is half as bad
As only knowing what

's gonna rope-a-dope, rope-a-dope
Dopin' up the shop
'Cuz the Baine damage got a package
From Corina Copp

Collie-collie, wiener dog
And cudgel up a cake
And a nine-and-twenty blackbird
Bobbin' on the lake

With an address! address!
Lolly gag amend! · Ya gotta
Gimme 'cuz the Post Office
Won't know where to send

And then the Winnemac, Winnemac
Waiting on a train · Ya gotta
Steam it open, ibuprofen!
Take away the pain

And then the Coelacanth, Coelacanth
Is sealing up the crack
And the catamaran | on top o' the man
Has nobody left to thank

Just like a tuna leg and Armantrout
And RAH RAH RAH
We are learning how to talk about
The AH HA HA

❧

SPIDER MONKEY GOT A HAIRCUT

Spider monkey got a haircut.
He sat down in the haircut chair.
I say to my kid: *At the first sight of tears,*
Your petition is denied.

An owl nurse came in with a speech impediment.
She couldn't say what she wanted.
The mouse put on the helmet.
The inside was little boxes.

Clear glass and how many colors.
Nobody could put on that helmet.
If I ask you to hand me a thing and you do it,
The words had nothing to do with it.

Here's a pair of jeans for you,
And a left-handed athlete for me.
The athlete needs to apply himself more.
The jeans were all right 'til they shrank.

Here's a pair of jeans for you,
And a left-handed athlete for me.
She misunderstood what you said? Not at all.
She got all there was to get.

Rain *isn't* as clever as snow.
Nor snow as smart as hail.
I *fled* that beautiful city
That makes you have to go numb.

The numbered sections are wrong a strawberry's
Taken control of the embassy.
That's how they knew it was Sin.
Just … whatever they repented.

The principal African animals
Are the lion, the witch, and the aardvark.
Best keep an eye on these Christians
Who don't believe in God.

I *think* I know a porpoise
From an out-of-work broke-ass dolphin.
I can't possibly be the protagonist
Or I'd be exempt from humiliation.

Dolphin, go to community college.
This dolphin's six months pregnant.
This is a source of dissatisfaction
For the ant, the gull, and the ant shark.

We leave you the Crystal of Truth.
But we're taking with us the Crystal of Fun.
You find out if you were an addict
The minute it's time to quit.

Inchworm over and over.
Maggot once or twice.
But merit is not merit enough:
There has to be pleasure…

Oh, inchworm, inchworm, inchworm.
And William Carlos Williams
Yelling into the open mouth
Of a nest of baby ostriches.

Water's made of molecules;
Molecules, out of atoms.
In therapy you can come to terms
With the millipede's indifference.

The magnetic strip on a debit card
Lets you be tracked from space.
A moment's the measure of time in which
Nothing at all can happen.

The airport has many hazards.
Impassable rivers and starvey wolves.
Their hunting patterns exactly match
Those of the stranded octopus.

And who *is* as the suckblob?
And who knoweth the interpretation of the suck?
Daddy Longlegs looked it up
In the Lithuanian textbook.

Oh, I know, I know, I know.
Interrupted a hundred times,
The psyche goes into crisis—and so:
Ineligible is the bat.

❧

FOX CALLED AND SANK A SHOT

Fox called and sank a shot
Into the corner pocket
Of a mock-Moroccan kangaroo
Who looked better naked.

She wanted to beat the snake to death
Without at all hurting the shovel.
She said "I'll teach you to speak out of turn,
Ya prig with a piña colada."

Ya anaconda swallowin' a story.
Ya platypus laying an egg.
See, you like judging others,
But you got cat food on your leg.

Pelican he got a stopwatch.
He clocking my every move.
We're like a sisal-bound bundle of antlers:
Irreconcilable differences.

Helluva dancer, that gila monster.
Looks great in a cotton body stocking.
But, talking shop with the audience, she's
As uptight as a scolding nannygoat.

Fitzgibbon the laughing hyena licked
The icing-encrusted spatula. He's all
Trying to put a nail in the wall
By hitting it with a mattress.

This ain't the Sixteenth Century.
It ain't the *Moriæ Encomium*.
The Sixteenth Century's "Song of Myself"
Was a list of ninety objections.

In orbit around the Earth we find
Innumerable frozen dead eagles.
Depend on it, Sir: When they divvy the spoils,
We get the bones and the feathers.

Anteater set up for a lecturer, paid out
A line and drew it back in. Arm-
adillo stepped over a sippy cup, threw
A seed in the sea and an island came up.

But me, as I crouch to pet this coil
Of orange extension cord, I think
Its mile-long flexible backbone
Is liquid metallic hydrogen.

So listen, you five (you two over there,
And you two, and this guy up front):
What's today? Mexican Monday.
Right, so it's time we lowered the boom.

Time we lowered the boom, and time
The reindeer electrician
Made his way through the rumpus room,
So he can set up his model of Saturn.

Poeckodat is Saturn.
Raemboe is the Moon.
Dieagnl stripes is Jupiter
And perpl is Uranus . . .

Oh, I know, I know, I know.
Well, I never said I wasn't! You
Rhinoceros standing in snow. You
Wringing-wet fed-up pheasant.

You polar bear selling Chiclets!
Yeah, bring it, I ain't scared.
In fact, I'm looking forward,
'Cuz you my buzzard, my BFF.

❧

.

ACKNOWLEDGMENTS

Grateful acknowledgment is made to the editors of the following journals in which some of these poems first appeared: *The Awl*, *Blackbox Manifold* (UK), *Blazing Stadium*, *B O D Y*, *Boston Review*, *Brooklyn Review*, *Columbia Poetry Review*, *Curator Magazine*, *Georgia Review*, *Iowa Review*, *Lana Turner*, *Leveler*, *Little Star*, *NONSITE*, *Poetry*, Poetry Foundation website, and *Tourniquet Review*.

Anthony Madrid was born in 1968, raised in Maryland. He is the author of three other full-length books of poetry: *I Am Your Slave Now Do What I Say* (Canarium Books, 2012), *Try Never* (Canarium Books, 2017), and *There Was an Old Man with a Springbok* (Prelude Books, 2019). He lives in Victoria, Texas with Nadya Pittendrigh.